Endangered Animals
of North America

Endangered Animals
of North America

A Hot Issue

David Goodnough

Enslow Publishers, Inc.

40 Industrial Road   PO Box 38
Box 398   Aldershot
Berkeley Heights, NJ 07922   Hants GU12 6BP
USA   UK

http://www.enslow.com

Library of Congress Cataloging-in-Publication Data

Goodnough, David.
    Endangered animals of North America : a hot issue / David
Goodnough.
        p. cm. — (Hot issues)
    Includes bibliographical references and index.
    Summary: Explores the problem of extinct and endangered
animals, the politics behind the issue, and ways of solving the
problem.
    ISBN 0-7660-1373-1 (hardcover)
    1. Endangered species—North America—Juvenile literature.
[1. Endangered species.] I. Title. II. Series.
QL83 .G664   2000
333.95'42'097—dc21
                                       00-009256

Printed in the United States of America

10 9 8 7 6 5 4 3 2 1

To Our Readers:
All Internet addresses in this book were active and appropriate when we
went to press. Any comments or suggestions can be sent by e-mail to
Comments@enslow.com or to the address on the back cover.

Illustration Credits: © Corel Corporation, pp. 3, 9, 12, 14, 19, 24,
30, 32, 41, 46, 47, 49, 50, 52, 56; Courtesy of Sagamore Hill National
Historic Site, National Park Service, p. 21.

Cover Illustration: © Corel Corporation

Contents

Chapter 1

The Problem

The American bald eagle is a large bird that was once common throughout the North American continent. Native Americans and, later, European colonists and settlers respected the eagle for both its size and its beauty. In 1782, the Congress of the United States passed an act making the bald eagle the national symbol of the young country. Its image would later appear on coins, postage stamps, and on the entrances to most government buildings. Yet within two centuries, bald eagles had almost disappeared in the United States, except in parts of the northwest and Alaska. Even there, their numbers were reduced to only a few hundred pairs of birds.[1]

Human beings caused most of this reduction in the eagle population. Native Americans hunted and trapped the eagle for its claws and feathers, which they used to decorate their headdresses and clothing. The early colonists and later settlers considered eagles a nuisance because they preyed on small animals that the farmers raised or hunted for food. The destruction of vast forest to make room for farms, roads, towns, and cities took away much of the natural environment, or habitat, in which the eagle lived and thrived.

Scientists now believe, however, that the greatest threat faced by the bald eagle was the use of chemical pesticides to control insects that were damaging farm products.[2] These chemicals entered the bodies of insects and small animals that were then eaten by eagles. The chemicals were stored in the body fat of eagles and interfered with the production of calcium. Eagles need calcium to harden the shells of their eggs. The birds' shells became so thin that they would break when the mother bird sat on them in the nest. As a result, the number of eagles that actually hatched became fewer and fewer.[3]

Scientists, animal lovers, concerned citizens, and politicians became worried that our national symbol would disappear from the land. The first federal law to protect the eagle was passed in 1940. This led to more laws protecting the eagle and providing aid for its survival. The most dangerous of the chemical pesticides, DDT, was banned from use in 1972. Now, after almost three decades of struggle to protect the bald eagle from pesticides and the destruction of its habitat, the nation has welcomed it back from near extinction. President Bill Clinton hailed the return of the bald eagle in his Fourth of July address to the nation in 1999: "It's hard to think of a better way to celebrate the birth of our nation than to celebrate the rebirth of our national symbol."[4]

The return of the bald eagle was a good reason to celebrate. However, the neglect and extinction of our wildlife is still a problem. And it is still a direct result of human interference in nature.

*T*he bald eagle, once near extinction, has recovered. However, most other endangered animals have not been as fortunate.

A Disappearance

At one time on the North American continent there were flocks of birds that blocked out the sun and stirred up a violent wind with the flutter of their wings. It would take many hours for them to pass over an area. These were passenger pigeons, fine examples of nature's abundance.[5] But in fewer than a hundred years, the passenger pigeon had vanished. Not a single one remains.

It is estimated that there were more than 5 billion passenger pigeons alive at any one time before the arrival of the European colonists in America.[6] It is almost impossible to believe that they were completely wiped out in less than a century. They were hunted and killed for food, as sport, or just because they were considered a nuisance.

The passenger pigeons' habit of flocking and nesting close to one another made them easy prey for hunters and sportsmen. A single professional hunter could kill almost five thousand pigeons in a single day, just by firing his shotgun into the circling flocks or catching them in nets. Trainloads of birds were sent to eastern cities for sale as food. In a single day, a New York merchant sold eighteen thousand pigeons to his customers.

In 1881, hunters removed twenty thousand baby pigeons from their nests and shipped them to New York to be shot in a Long Island "pigeon shoot." This event was sponsored by the New York State Association for the Protection of Fish and Game. In 1822, one family in Chautauqua, New York, killed four thousand pigeons because they wanted to use the birds' feathers as decorations on hats.[7]

The common attitude was that it would be impossible to kill them all. Even lawmakers agreed.

In 1857, the Ohio Senate refused to pass a law to control the slaughter. And yet, in just a few decades they would be gone forever. The last passenger pigeon died in 1914, in a Cincinnati zoo.[8]

A Comeback

The passenger pigeon shared the continent with an equal abundance of prairie dogs. These small rodents lived in burrows, or tunnels, in the rich lands of the Midwest and West. An underground village of prairie dogs could cover an area 100 miles wide and 250 miles long and might contain 400 million prairie dogs.[9] Farmers and ranchers hated them because they ate nearly all the plant life in any area they occupied. They robbed the grazing farm animals of their food supply. Their burrows also were a constant danger to horses or cattle who might step in them and break their legs.

Beginning in 1900, prairie dog villages were being systematically destroyed by poisoning and plowing. By 1950, the prairie dog colonies had been greatly reduced in ranching areas. It appeared that the prairie dog was headed for extinction. Another animal affected was the black-footed ferret, a rare weasel-like animal that eats prairie dogs. The ferret could not live without the prairie dog, so it too seemed likely to be destroyed. These two animals have since made a comeback, through the efforts of conservationists and citizens concerned with the lives and well-being of animals.

The Buffalo

The largest North American animal that existed in such incredible numbers was the American bison, or buffalo. There were once around 50 million of

*B*y the mid-1900s, prairie dogs were nearly extinct. Conservationists worked hard to save them, and they have made a comeback.

them on the Great Plains, stretching from the Mississippi River westward to the Rocky Mountains. No one knows how many existed east of the Mississippi before the arrival of European colonists.

Buffalo had always been hunted by American Indians because they were so useful. The American Indians ate buffalo meat raw or cooked, and dried it for use in the winter. They used its skin for clothing and on tepees for shelter. They used its bones to make tools and weapons. There was very little of the buffalo that they did not use. They hunted the buffalo on foot with spears or bows and arrows. Sometimes they were able to force them to stampede over cliffs, obtaining a rich harvest of meat and skins from the slain animals. Even though they hunted buffalo regularly, they made little dent in the total number. There were simply too few American Indians to endanger the large population of buffalo.

All of that changed with the arrival of European explorers and colonists, beginning in the 1500s. The Spanish explorers brought horses with them, which the Southwest and Plains Indians quickly learned how to use and ride. They were now able to run the buffalo down and shoot them with their arrows. The Dutch, English, and French colonists brought firearms with them, which the American Indians were also quick to learn how to use. They now had a tremendous advantage over the buffalo, but they still had great respect for it. The buffalo was at the center of their culture. The American Indians depended on the buffalo for food and other necessary supplies.

The Europeans, however, saw the buffalo as merely a source of food, profit, or sport. With the coming of settlers and the railroads to the Plains in

*N*early 50 million buffalo once roamed the Great Plains. By 1870, the great herds of buffalo were gone. The animals had been killed either for sport or for profit.

the 1800s, the buffalo became a problem. The great herds blocked the passage of trains and became a nuisance to travelers and settlers. Professional hunters were hired to kill as many buffalo as they could. This was done both to supply food for railroad construction crews and to keep the herds from wandering onto the tracks. The famous buffalo hunter Buffalo Bill Cody was hired by the Kansas Pacific Railroad. Expeditions of sportsmen were organized to shoot the buffalo for pleasure and for trophies. Buffalo hunting became one of the main industries of the Plains. By 1870, the great herds of buffalo had vanished. What was left were huge heaps of bones and rotting flesh. A few stragglers remained, but for all practical purposes, the buffalo was gone.

Other Animals at Risk

If animals that existed in such large numbers could be wiped out so easily, what chance did other, less numerous animals have? Not much, if they got in the way of human beings or were considered useful to humans. The beaver was nearly eliminated because of the value of its skin in Europe, where it was used to make men's hats. Rare birds were slain for their colorful feathers, which were used to decorate ladies' hats and clothing. The pronghorn, or American antelope, was hunted not only for its meat but also for sport. It is one of America's fastest and most beautiful animals, and its mounted head became a valued trophy for the hunter. The same was true of elk and moose.

Most of this destruction of wildlife took place in the 1700s and 1800s. It was brought about with bow and arrow, rifle and shotgun, poison, explosives, and traps. Since then, much more destructive agents have affected natural resources in the United States. Polluting an animal's habitat can greatly reduce that animal's population. Eliminating habitats, through overdevelopment or other means, can also cause a significant reduction in an animal's numbers. Modern methods of disease control for crops and vegetation can rid the world of as many animals as plant diseases. Any of these may result in extinction. All are the result of human activity, and animals are defenseless against them.

Destruction of animal habitats is happening all across the world. Many biologists believe that we are experiencing a worldwide mass extinction of living things. This mass extinction is perhaps the largest and the fastest in Earth's 4.5-billion-year history. Scientists warn that this loss of animal life will eventually be a threat to human existence.[10] However, many people are unaware of this loss of animal life and its possible effects on the United States and its population.

In 1966, the United States Interior Department created a list of Endangered and Threatened Species within the United States. A species is a type of plant or animal that usually reproduces only with its own kind. The current list includes more than one thousand plant and animal species—and is growing at the rate of approximately eighty-five additional species per year.[11] Some scientists consider this potential loss of species a more serious threat to human existence than all other global issues, including depletion of the ozone layer, global warming, overpopulation, and pollution and contamination of the environment. They believe that it is a major international crisis that calls for immediate action. Solutions offered include stronger state and national laws and individual action by citizens. Scientists, environmentalists, and concerned public officials are calling on us to make changes in our daily lives. They are asking us to help save these creatures from extinction.

Chapter 2

From Destruction to Conservation

Before European explorers and settlers came to the North American continent, the main dangers animals faced were natural forces. Aside from the diseases spread by parasites, viruses, and bacteria, animals fell prey to other animals—predators. Natural catastrophes such as forest fires, droughts, floods, volcanic eruptions, and earthquakes also took their toll on animal life. After the exploration and settlement of the continent, however, animals faced a far greater danger: men intent on food, financial gain, or sport. In the years following the Civil War (1860–1865), the slaughter of wildlife in the United States reached its peak.[1]

Worried Citizens

A few organizations, such as the Audubon Society, formed of scientists, private citizens, and politicians, became alarmed at the rapid destruction of the nation's wildlife. They began to petition state and federal officials for the protection of animals and their natural environments. Their first real accomplishment was to get the government to establish Yellowstone National Park in 1872. This first national park was intended to be a wildlife preserve, not a tourist attraction. It was here that the last large herd of buffalo was allowed to roam, free of danger from being hunted. The only danger the buffalo faced was from their natural predators, such as wolves, which were also protected within the park.

Animal-friendly groups also wanted laws passed to establish definite, limited seasons for the hunting of big game such as deer, elk, and pronghorn. Several states began to pass laws that protected wildlife within their borders. In 1876, the federal Forest Reserve Bill was passed by Congress. This bill was intended to protect only government-owned forests around river sources. But it showed that the government was in favor of preserving natural environments and the wildlife living in them.

In 1883, a group of scientists who studied birds founded the American Ornithologists' Union (AOU). Their goal was to protect what was left of America's rare birds and to promote the study of birds. The AOU has grown into one of the country's most important conservation societies. In 1885, a private organization was founded by George Bird Grinnell to protest the slaughter of birds for their feathers. This later grew into the National Audubon Society, which is now one of the most important and strongest forces in the fight to preserve and protect wildlife and the environment.[2]

These and other organizations and societies fought a ceaseless but almost unknown battle against the hunters, sportsmen, and builders who were turning the nation's forests and streams into money-making enterprises. Then, in the early 1890s, a group of poachers, or illegal hunters, invaded Yellowstone National Park. They managed to avoid

Yellowstonc National Park was established in 1872 as a wildlife preserve. Pictured here are the Yellowstone Falls.

the park rangers and began killing the last herd of buffalo in the country. Conservation groups protested loudly, and the general public became aware of the problem. In 1900, the government finally responded to public pressure and passed the Lacey Act. This act was sponsored by Representative John Lacey of Iowa.[3]

The Government Steps In

The Lacey Act was the government's first effort at true wildlife management. The act made it a crime to transport illegally killed animals from one state into another state. This may not sound like much, but it helped to put many poachers out of business. It also gave the Department of Agriculture the authority to enforce the law. The Department of Agriculture is one of the most important departments of the government, so the states took it very seriously.

When Theodore Roosevelt became president of the United States in 1901, the conservation movement finally had a friend in power. President Roosevelt was an outdoorsman and sportsman who loved to hunt and fish. However, he respected and appreciated wildlife. He also had many friends among the founders of the Audubon Society and other conservation groups. As a private citizen he had been a powerful voice in urging the creation of national parks and wildlife preserves.

Once in office, President Roosevelt aided in the establishment of the U.S. Forest Service. He also created the nation's first national wildlife refuge in Pelican Island, Florida. This was another early step in the creation of our present system of national parks and wildlife preserves.[4] The public welcomed these projects. Although it was too late to save the passenger pigeon, the buffalo and other threatened animals were saved from extinction with this government aid.

However, there were now some new dangers to animals that would prove to be far more destructive than any hunter with a bow and arrow or a gun.

*T*heodore Roosevelt, pictured here with his family in 1903, had a deep respect for nature and wildlife. As president of the United States, Roosevelt helped establish the U.S Forest Service and created the country's first national wildlife refuge.

Chapter 3

The Greatest Threats

The achievements of the early conservation movement had convinced people that the problem was solved. They felt all that was needed to preserve endangered animals was to provide legal protection from hunters and poachers, set aside national parks and preserves where animals could roam freely, and help animals survive natural disasters. Most people felt that animals could take care of themselves if left alone by human beings. It was not until the 1920s that conservationists began to change their thinking about how to protect wildlife.

An Experiment Goes Wrong

Some animals, such as deer, had been nearly wiped out in the previous century. However, they were now making a comeback. Deer were the favorite prey of animals such as wolves, mountain lions, bobcats, and coyotes. To help the deer along, a predator-control program was begun by the Forest Service. In one area, the Kaibab Plateau in northern Arizona, more than six hundred mountain lions, the chief predator of deer, were killed. The deer herd in the Kaibab, now protected from humans as well as other animals, nearly tripled in size in only six years. Ten years later, in 1922, the much larger herd had again more than doubled in size. The only trouble was that the Kaibab Plateau did not have enough plant life to feed this huge herd. The deer stripped the area bare. Soon they began to wander outside their natural environment in search of food. To wildlife observers, this was a sign of overpopulation. The U.S. Forest Service tried to reduce the herd by calling for a special hunt in the Kaibab but was accused by the state of Arizona of intruding on that state's right to deal with such matters in its own way. The matter went to court, while thousands of deer died of starvation in the severe winters that the area experienced in the late 1920s.[1]

Land Management

Some animal lovers opposed any thinning of the herd and argued that the Kaibab was a special case. This argument was proved wrong when evidence came in from other parts of the country where the deer population was exploding. One person familiar with the deer problem was a man named Aldo Leopold. Leopold, a teacher, had held different jobs dealing with wildlife. At one time he had believed that eliminating predators was the solution to saving dwindling animal life. He now saw that he was wrong. He changed his viewpoint entirely. "Conservation is a state of harmony between men and land," he wrote in his book *Game Management*. "By land is meant all the things on, over, or in the earth."[2] He was one of the first to note that changing the environment would affect—for good or bad— the lives of the various animals living in that environment. "We have learned," he wrote, "that game is a crop, which Nature will grow and grow abundantly, provided only we furnish the seed and suitable environment."[3] Leopold's writings and teachings were taken seriously. He is regarded as one of the most influential leaders of the conservation movement during the mid-1900s.

Habitat Destruction

To Leopold, the "environment" included all of the animals living in any particular spot on the earth. The term was too broad to account for the situation of any particular animal, so today we speak of an

*I*n some habitats, predators like the bobcat are necessary to keep the population of deer and other species under control. Removing a species' natural predators leads to overpopulation. Overpopulation then leads to food shortages, because the animals eat all available plant life.

animal's habitat rather than environment. An animal's habitat is the surroundings in which it is usually found, whether in forests, deserts, plains, or wetlands. An animal's habitat is necessary for that animal's survival.

Most biologists, conservationists, and wildlife managers agree that habitat change or destruction is the greatest danger to animal life.[4] Unfortunately, habitat change or destruction is mainly the result of human activity. This may appear obvious now, but in earlier times, human activity seemed mild compared to earthquakes, volcanic eruptions, hurricanes, floods, and other natural disasters. In the past few centuries, human activity has increased to such an extent that it often plays a more significant role in habitat change than natural disasters do. Also, a habitat can usually recover from a natural disaster, such as an earthquake. It cannot, however, recover from an airport, a superhighway, or a shopping mall.

In 1998, the American Institute of Biological Sciences ranked the causes of habitat destruction.[5] First is agriculture. Agriculture often involves clearing the land of forests, draining wetlands, building dams and canals for irrigation, and destroying animals, birds, or insects that may prevent healthy crop growth. In recent times, the use of pesticides and herbicides has made some habitats dangerous not only to animals but to humans as well.

Second is commercial development. This includes anything from logging operations to building industrial parks, large areas set aside for industrial use. Commercial development is a human activity that has increased greatly in the last two centuries. Mining operations have completely destroyed whole environments, not just the habitats

MISSING

These animals once existed in great numbers.

Atlantic gray whale	Location: Atlantic Ocean. Last seen: 1750. (The Pacific gray whale has recovered.)
Great auk	Location: North Atlantic seaboard. Last seen: 1844.
Badlands bighorn sheep	Location: Upper Great Plains. Last seen: 1910.
Passenger pigeon	Location: Midwest. Last seen: 1914.
Florida red wolf	Location: Florida. Last seen: 1925. (Believed to have interbred with coyotes.)
Silver trout	Location: Western New Hampshire. Last seen: 1930.
Heath hen	Location: Martha's Vineyard, Massachusetts. Last seen: 1932.
Santa Barbara song sparrow	Location: Santa Barbara Island, California. Last seen: 1959.
Blue pike	Location: Lake Erie. Last seen: 1971.
Dusky seaside sparrow	Location: Florida. Last seen: 1987.
Ivory-billed woodpecker	Location: Eastern forests. No recent sightings.

Source: Douglas H. Chadwick and Joel Sartore, *The Company We Keep: America's Endangered Species* (Washington, D.C.: National Geographic Society, 1996).

within them. New housing developments gobble up huge areas of land.

The third major cause of habitat destruction is water development, which affects mostly aquatic animals. Building dams, canals, and levees (large earth embankments built to prevent rivers from flooding) affects larger animals by diverting their water supply, cutting through their territories, separating them from resources on which they may depend, or simply flooding their habitat.

The fourth major cause involves the development and maintenance of our infrastructure. The infrastructure of a nation includes its systems of communication, transportation, and public services, as well as its military facilities. In terms of threatening the habitats of endangered animals, chief among these is the system of roads and highways. This system may be considered necessary, but it is also highly destructive to wildlife habitats.

There are many other human activities that cause habitat destruction, but they can usually be grouped under the four main causes. Extractive land use (activities that take away natural materials from a habitat) can usually be grouped under agriculture or commercial development. Examples of extractive land use are mining, logging, and grazing. Outdoor recreation, including the use of off-road vehicles, can also destroy habitat. Such activities can be considered part of commercial development.

These activities contribute to the well-being of the human population. They are not likely to be stopped. In some cases, they cannot even be regulated without long and bitter legal struggles between those people who want to preserve the land and those who want to use it for their own gain or pleasure. This has brought about the present crisis, in which it appears that we are headed for a mass extinction of many of the living creatures on this planet.[6] The problem is how to prevent this extinction and at the same time continue with our human activities.

Chapter 4

The Politics of Endangerment

In the late 1920s and early 1930s, wildlife observers began to notice a sharp drop in the waterfowl population of the northern midwest United States and central Canada. Many conservation organizations had worked to protect the migrating flocks of ducks and geese that were so common to these areas. The Migratory Bird Treaty Act of 1918 had placed limits on hunting and tried to ensure that all types of waterfowl would have a decent chance to survive and reproduce without serious danger from humans.[1]

Human Needs

Despite all the laws and goodwill on the part of hunters, lawmakers, and animal lovers, the waterfowl population began to decline. Human needs had brought about swamp drainage, canal and dam construction, and stream diversion. These actions reduced the wetlands that were the natural habitat of waterfowl. The Bear River Marshes of Utah, for example, were almost completely dried up.

For centuries, the Bear River Marshes had been one of the continent's most densely populated waterfowl areas. Large numbers of waterfowl were still drawn to the dwindling wetlands. The marshes became so crowded that diseases spread rapidly among the flocks. These diseases were caused by the now-polluted waters of the marshes, which were breeding grounds for deadly germs that infected thousands of birds.[2]

Wildlife experts and conservationists knew what was happening. They did everything they could to restore the marshes. They even managed to get Congress to pass the Migratory Bird Conservation Act, which was intended to protect wetlands as refuges for wildfowl.[3] This was a step in the right direction. Unfortunately the year was 1929, the start of the Great Depression, which troubled the nation for the next ten years. This was a period in which business, agriculture, employment, and living conditions declined to a very low level. The American people became more interested in preserving themselves and their families than in saving wildlife. To make things worse, the year 1931 was especially dry, with a drastic decrease in rainfall. Many parts of the country were turned into waterless wastelands. Rivers as well as wetlands dried up. The drought was as devastating to people as it was to wildlife.

The Government Takes Charge

When Franklin D. Roosevelt was elected president in 1932, he recommended to Congress a vast range of programs. These programs were designed to help the people as well as the land recover from the Great Depression and the drought. Known as the New Deal, these programs helped put the nation on the road to recovery. In addition to helping people recover financially from the Great Depression in general, it

*T*he government attempted to save fragile wetland habitats by passing the Migratory Bird Conservation Act in 1929. Preservation and restoration of wetlands continues to be an important issue even today.

helped farmers recover land that had been lost due to poor farming practices in the past. New life was breathed into the conservation movement.

Roosevelt's secretary of the interior, Harold L. Ickes, was a dedicated conservationist. With his encouragement and leadership, the Wilderness Society was organized in 1934. In 1935, the American Wildlife Institute was started. These organizations had great influence through their publications and their efforts to educate the public on the importance of conserving natural resources and protecting wildlife. The aim was to maintain balance between human needs and preserving the environment.

World War II (1941–1945) proved to be another

setback for conservation and wildlife management in the United States. With most park rangers and wildlife managers serving in the armed forces, there was not enough man- or womanpower left to oversee the nation's natural resources—land, forests, water, and wildlife. All of the nation's energies were directed toward winning the war.

World War II ended in 1945, but the nation was soon plunged into other conflicts, starting with the Cold War against Russia and continuing with the Korean War (1950–1953). President Dwight D. Eisenhower was committed to winning both of these wars. He was also cautious when it came to land and resource management. The secretary of the interior under Eisenhower, Douglas McKay, believed that private companies rather than government agencies should control the nation's resources.

During his two years in office, McKay allowed private businesses to exploit the wildlife refuges. He appointed politicians to jobs that were formerly held by experienced wildlife managers. As a result, morale in these services was low. Many well-trained wildlife workers resigned.

McKay retired in 1955, and the situation immediately improved under the new secretary of the interior, Fred Seaton. Congress passed the Fish and Wildlife Act in 1956. This act paved the way for the formation of a new United States Fish and Wildlife Service, which is now responsible for most of the work done by the government to save endangered animals.[4]

New Dangers

However, things did not get any better for wildlife. The widespread use of deadly insecticides such as

DDT, increased industrial waste and pollution, and huge increases in human population were threatening the natural environment as never before. Added to these was the danger of nuclear fallout from the testing of atomic weapons.

In 1962, Rachel Carson published *Silent Spring*. She argued that the uncontrolled use of chemicals to kill insects was also killing the world's birds. Songbirds would no longer be heard, and the calls of wild geese and ducks would vanish forever. Many scientists and all chemical manufacturers scoffed at her warning. They attacked her as being unscientific. But it soon became obvious that she was right. The bald eagle, the national symbol of the United States, began to disappear, even though it

*T*he bald eagle is the national symbol of the United States. Its image is often found on the country's coins, stamps, and government buildings.

was protected by federal laws from hunters and its nesting areas were declared refuges. The peregrine falcon, once so common in the northeastern states that it nested in bridges and skyscrapers, became so reduced in number that it disappeared east of the Mississippi River. The osprey, or fish hawk, population was also drastically reduced.

Investigators found that the one thing these birds had in common was a high level of pesticides in their systems. The main culprit was DDT, a powerful insecticide (insect-killing chemical). The pesticides had been picked up by the birds from the food they ate—rodents, fish, insects, and other small animals. These smaller animals had either been sprayed with pesticides themselves or had eaten plants or other organisms that were sprayed.

These chemicals interfered with the birds' ability to produce eggshells. The eggs they laid had such thin shells that they broke when the birds sat on them during the incubation period. The evidence against the harmful effects of DDT was so strong that in 1972 the government banned its use. Since then, the bald eagle, the peregrine falcon, and the osprey have staged a comeback. It is hoped that other animal and wildfowl species will also recover from their deadly exposure to dangerous pesticides.

When John F. Kennedy became president in 1961, conservation and wildlife management took on a new look. President Kennedy appointed Stewart Udall, a former senator from Utah, as secretary of the interior. The new secretary was an energetic and outspoken champion for the preservation of natural resources and the protection of wildlife. His 1963 book, *The Quiet Crisis*, brought

"The Billion-Dollar Bird"

The northern spotted owl's habitat is in the Pacific Northwest, the heart of the logging industry. When the spotted owl was put on the endangered list, the loggers in the area were banned from working in the huge forests that cover the area. The outcry from the loggers was loud and angry. Thousands of jobs would be lost, they claimed, and it would cost the economy billions of dollars. "We're endangered," they cried. The issue was finally settled by the Supreme Court in 1994, and the spotted owl was the winner. The dispute is not over. Companies are still lobbying for amendments and changes to the Endangered Species Act that would allow logging operations to return to the undisturbed forest habitat of the spotted owl.

Source: Douglas H. Chadwick and Joel Sartore, *The Company We Keep: America's Endangered Species* (Washington, D.C.: National Geographic Society, 1996).

public attention to a great danger facing the planet's animals and people—human overpopulation.

As the number of people on Earth increases, human needs increase. More land is used for housing. More wetlands are drained to make way for airports, factories, and shopping malls. More highways are built for the millions of cars that drive on our streets—and pollute the air. Industries dump more poisonous wastes into our rivers. Our whole environment, wrote Udall, is being battered from every side as more and more demands on it are made to satisfy human needs.[5]

Congress Acts

Supported by the president and the secretary of the interior, Congress suddenly began to make real attempts to improve the situation. The Clean Air Act was passed in 1963. It limits the amount of pollutants that industries can release into the air. Animal protection laws, such as the Wilderness Act in 1964 and the National Environmental Policy Act in 1969, strengthened laws already in place. These acts gave more power to wildlife agencies and organizations and new life to the conservation movement.

All of this came to a head in 1970 with the celebration of the first Earth Day on April 22. Teach-ins were held at schools and colleges to inform the public about environmental problems. Cleanup campaigns were held throughout the country. Earth Day has become a yearly national celebration of the environment. It reminds people of the need for clean air, clear water, and productive land that can support wildlife as well as human life.

Voters' growing concern over the preservation of the environment and the protection of wildlife influenced lawmakers in Congress. In 1973, they passed the controversial Endangered Species Act, which amounted to a Bill of Rights for wildlife and plants. The groundwork for this act had been laid in 1966, when Congress passed the Endangered Species Preservation Act. This act directed the secretary of the interior to furnish a list of native animals that were in danger of extinction and to take steps to ensure their survival.

The Department of the Interior named eighty-three species of wildlife that were in danger of disappearing. Among them were the grizzly bear, the blue whale, the California condor, and the black-footed ferret. But since there were hardly any funds or governmental powers granted to carry out this task, the act had little effect.

An expansion of the act in 1969 added reptiles (animals with scales, such as lizards and snakes), amphibians (animals capable of living both on land and in water, such as frogs), mollusks (animals with soft bodies covered with shells, such as clams), and crustaceans (animals that live chiefly in the water and have legs and bodies covered by shells, such as lobsters and crabs) to the list when any of them became threatened or endangered. This step was taken mainly because poachers were illegally trapping alligators and had almost wiped them out. Again, no funds or powers were given to make the act any more effective. Not a single species was added to the endangered list between 1970 and 1973. However, the expansion of the list showed a growing public awareness of how many species there are and how the extinction of one could affect another.

The Endangered Species Act

The Endangered Species Act (ESA) of 1973 changed all that. It faced the threat of extinction squarely and spelled out what was at stake: "The Congress finds and declares that various species of fish, wildlife, and plants in the United States have been rendered extinct. . . ."[6] It goes on to say that this was the result of economic growth and development that went on without concern for conservation. It talked of other species in danger of extinction. It also noted that the United States, as a part of the international community, has pledged to preserve as far as

Highlights of the
Endangered Species Act (1973)

The Congress finds and declares that:

(1) various species of fish, wildlife, and plants in the United States have been rendered extinct as a consequence of economic growth and development untempered by adequate concern and conservation;

(2) other species of fish, wildlife, and plants have been so depleted in numbers that they are in danger of, or threatened with, extinction;

(3) these species of fish, wildlife, and plants are of esthetic, ecological, educational, historical, recreational, and scientific value to the Nation and its people;

(4) the United States has pledged itself as a sovereign state in the international community to conserve to the extent practicable the various species of fish or wildlife and plants facing extinction. . . .

Source: Endangered Species Act (ESA) of 1973. A full text of the ESA can be obtained on the Internet at <http://www.fws.gov> (August 14, 2000).

possible "the various species of fish or wildlife and plants facing extinction."[7]

It is notable that plants were included for the first time. This was further recognition that all of nature is connected. It meant that not only would certain animals be protected but also the environment they depended on to live. The act would be overseen and enforced by the Fish and Wildlife Service, which would also be given a large annual budget to carry out its aims.

The ESA also insisted that the selection of endangered animals would be based on the best scientific information available, and that there would be no economic considerations. This turned out to be one of the most criticized and debated parts of the act. The logging and mining industries, ranchers, and oil and gas companies felt that they were being treated unfairly. It would be impossible, for example, to carry on a logging operation without disturbing the habitat of birds and small animals such as squirrels.

The act also stated that all federal agencies would do their best to protect endangered species. This meant that all public works such as highways, dams, and bridges would be affected. Congressmen became involved if such public works were needed by their states. Communities that could have bene-fited from a new interstate highway or bridge were angered when the planned construction came under review by the Fish and Wildlife Service. Newspapers, business groups, and workers made their feelings known, and their congressmen lis-tened. Polls showed, however, that at least two thirds of the public supported the ESA and would be willing to pay more in taxes to support it.[8]

Even though the ESA is supported by most congressmen and by most of the general public, it has been under fire for most of its existence. Amendments, or changes, have been added over the years that softened its hard stand. A 1992 amendment was an attempt by the government to satisfy powerful critics of the ESA, such as real estate interests and ranching and logging groups. Under this amendment, large property owners are free to develop a portion of their land in exchange for leaving other portions protected. Such arrangements are called Habitat Conservation Plans (HCP). Under a so-called "no surprises" clause in the amendment, landowners are assured that they will not have to change any part of their arrangement, even though scientific evidence may show that endangered animals are declining because of changing conditions in the environment. Most conservationists and wildlife managers regard "no surprises" as a death warrant to animals that are on the brink of extinction.[9]

Chapter 5

Some Successes

In 1998, the Fish and Wildlife Service proudly announced that about two dozen animals were to be taken off the Department of the Interior's Endangered and Threatened Species List. Among the animals dropped from the list were the gray wolf, the Colombian white-tailed deer, the bald eagle, the Aleutian Canada goose, and the brown pelican. Critics pointed out that more than one hundred species were waiting to be added to the list and that the list was growing at the rate of eighty-five species a year.[1] Still, it was an enormous achievement when compared to the situation that existed before the passage of the Endangered Species Act in 1973. Here are some of the animals that have almost recovered from their endangered state.

The Gray Wolf

The wolf had never been a popular animal with people. In Europe it is associated with viciousness and evil. This is the image found in many fairy tales and in the myth of the werewolf. The early colonists brought this prejudice with them. The wolf was either killed or driven out of the eastern part of the country.

Ranchers and cattlemen in the West saw the wolf as a danger to their flocks and herds. The pursuit and destruction of the wolf was sometimes ruthless. In 1905, cattlemen forced the state of Montana to pass a law requiring the state veterinarian to infect captive wolves and then release them to spread disease among the wolf population.[2] Ten years later, ranchers and cattlemen lobbied Congress to have wolves removed from all lands owned by the government.

The gray wolf was added to the endangered list in 1974. However, any steps to protect or increase its

*T*he gray wolf is one of the success stories of the conservation movement. Although it was placed on the Endangered Species List in 1974, the gray wolf is slowly making a comeback. Breeding pairs are being released into the wild and the animal seems to be recovering in the northwest.

numbers brought a storm of complaints. In spite of this, about ten breeding pairs of gray wolves were released in Idaho, eight in Yellowstone Park, and ten in Montana. So far the wolf seems to have recovered in the northwest. It is scheduled to be taken off the endangered list before the year 2002.

The gray wolf has not been so lucky in the southwest. Eleven wolves that had been bred in captivity were released in eastern Arizona in the spring of 1997. In November 1998, the last remaining gray wolf was found dead, apparently from natural causes. This ended the first effort to return the wolf to the wilds of the desert states.[3]

Why bring the gray wolf back in the first place? First, of course, is that it has been a part of the environment in the western United States since before recorded history. Second, it is one of the great predators, keeping the balance of large species such as deer and buffalo. Third, in the words of *Audubon* magazine, "It's enough to know they're out there again, part of the ancient equation that makes wild, beautiful places whole and healthy."[4]

The Wild Turkey

When the Pilgrims of Massachusetts celebrated the first Thanksgiving in 1620, they dined on wild turkey. It was one of the most common game birds and seemed to be everywhere. Benjamin Franklin proposed that the wild turkey should be our national symbol instead of the bald eagle. The wild turkey, he argued, is a great benefit to humankind, while the bald eagle is a predator. By the twentieth century, however, the wild turkey population had been reduced by more than 99 percent, which meant that it was nearly extinct. Unrestricted hunting and

RECOVERED!

These animals are no longer considered endangered.

✔ **Rydberg milk-vetch**

✔ **Palau dove**

✔ **Palau owl**

✔ **Palau fantail flycatcher**

✔ **Brown pelican**

✔ **Arctic peregrine falcon**

✔ **American alligator**

✔ **Gray whale**

Source: Douglas H. Chadwick and Joel Sartore, *The Company We Keep: America's Endangered Species* (Washington, D.C.: National Geographic Society, 1996).

clearing of the vast forests that were its habitat were the main causes.

Some state agencies undertook attempts to restore the wild turkey for the benefit of hunters. But these efforts met with little success. The problem was that the birds released into the wild were birds that had been raised in captivity. They failed to adapt in the wild. Wildlife managers then tried trapping wild birds, breeding them, and rereleasing them into their habitat. This method was so successful that the recovery of the wild turkey has been called one of the greatest success stories of wildlife management. Today there are probably more wild turkeys in America than there were when the pilgrims first landed on these shores. They exist in every state except Alaska. This is amazing, since it had never been recorded that they were ever seen before in the Far West.[5]

The Black-Footed Ferret

The black-footed ferret is a curious case, since its survival depends on another animal's survival. This rare, weasel-like animal is the only ferret native to the United States. For its food, it depends entirely on the prairie dogs of the Great Plains. When the prairie dog became threatened, the much scarcer black-footed ferret became endangered. By 1979, the ferret was thought to be extinct. Two years later, however, a ranch dog killed a ferret in Wyoming. Twelve others were found and caught, but six of them died after being taken out of their natural environment. The Fish and Wildlife Service decided to launch a campaign to save the ferret. By breeding them in captivity, it managed to raise almost one thousand ferrets. These ferrets were later released in an area stretching from Montana to Arizona.[6]

The black-footed ferret's troubles are not over yet. It still depends on the prairie dog as its main source of food, and the prairie dog is still making trouble for the farmers and ranchers of the Midwest. After the prairie dog made its comeback from near extinction in the 1940s and 1950s, it went right back to doing what it had always done. It ate all the ground plants it could hold and burrowed into the earth, creating vast prairie dog cities just below the surface. Cows and horses again stepped into the prairie dogs' burrows, breaking their legs or throwing their riders. Ranchers and farmers also went back to doing what they had always done. They began killing off the prairie dogs. It is expected that the Fish and Wildlife Service will soon declare the prairie dog an endangered species again. Part of the reason for this is that the prairie dog is necessary for the black-footed ferret's survival.[7]

The Sea Otter

Although the sea otter is awkward and slow on land, it is sleek and swift in the water. It feeds on a variety of shellfish, which it scoops up from the ocean floor. One of the most delightful sights in nature is the sea otter swimming on its back, cracking the shells of its meal on a flat rock it has placed on its stomach.

Sea otter fur has long been valued by hunters. The sea otter was hunted so widely in the last century that it was nearly wiped out of existence. When the otter disappears from an area, sea urchins, one of the otter's favorite foods, take over and feed on kelp. Kelp, a type of seaweed, provides food for a wide variety of fish and wildlife. When the sea urchin eats the kelp, the balance of the environment is upset. When the otter is returned to such an area, the balance is soon restored.

The otter has been protected since the earliest days of the conservation movement. But even though it was protected, the otter seemed to disappear. Then, in 1938, a group of ninety-four otters was sighted off Monterey, California. Since then, with protection and with the relocation of captured animals, the otter has thrived, particularly in northern Pacific waters. It has done so well that

*T*he sea otter, valued by hunters for its fur, was nearly hunted to extinction in the last century. Successful recovery efforts have helped the sea otter thrive again.

otter hunting is now permitted in Alaska, under strict state control.[8]

The Grizzly Bear

The most fearsome animal Lewis and Clark met on their expedition to the West in 1805 was the grizzly bear. These huge predators are very aggressive and will attack humans if they are threatened. The grizzly ranged over most of western North America and as far east as Minnesota. Naturally, they came into contact with the early settlers, who would not tolerate such a dangerous animal. Since grizzlies attacked large animals such as cattle and sheep, they were hated by ranchers and herdsmen. The hunting of grizzlies soon took its toll. Over the years, the grizzlies' number was reduced from between fifty thousand and one hundred thousand to fewer than one thousand in the United States, except for Alaska.[9]

The grizzly was declared threatened in 1975. Steps were taken to save it. Undeveloped areas of the country were set aside for the bears to live. The best known of these is Yellowstone National Park. Grizzlies became a common sight to tourists at the park when the bears began raiding garbage dumps for food.

To save grizzly bears from extinction, undeveloped areas of the country have been set aside for them to live. One of the best known homes of the grizzly bear is Yellowstone National Park.

In 1968, wildlife experts decided that the bears were becoming too dependent on garbage dumps as their source of food and were getting too close to humans. They closed the dumps, thus forcing the grizzlies to hunt for their food. Today, the grizzly population seems stable.

Grizzlies have caused deaths to humans in Yellowstone and in other grizzly country areas. Why protect such a dangerous animal? Some wildlife experts claim that the grizzly is an "umbrella" species. Protecting the grizzly's habitat helps many other animals. Other people believe that the grizzly, like the gray wolf, is a living symbol of the wilderness and the wild places that are becoming rarer each day.[10]

The Bald Eagle and the Peregrine Falcon

Two of the great success stories of the endangered species movement are the bald eagle and the peregrine falcon. Both were victims of habitat destruction and DDT poisoning. When DDT was banned by the government in 1972, these birds were given a fighting chance for survival. Their chances were greatly improved by the actions of two groups. The National Audubon Society not only helped to ban DDT but waged a national campaign of publicity and education to bring attention to the plight of the bald eagle. The Peregrine Fund contributed large sums of money for a captive-breeding program. The group also protected young birds that were released in the wild. Today both species have been taken off the endangered list.[11]

*T*he peregrine falcon is no longer on the Endangered Species List. The ban on DDT by the United States government in 1972 was an important factor in its recovery.

The Pronghorn and the White-Tailed Deer

"Home on the range, where the deer and the antelope play," says the old American song. But by the beginning of the twentieth century, the deer and the pronghorn antelope that once crowded the plains and forests had practically vanished. Pronghorns, which at one time outnumbered buffalo, were down to fewer than fifteen thousand animals by 1915. A decline in the sheep industry, which opened up grazing land that had been guarded by dogs and shepherds, allowed a slight recovery for pronghorns. Hunting regulations and

*A*t the beginning of the twentieth century, there were fewer than fifteen thousand pronghorn antelope left in the United States. Due to new hunting regulations and changes in the sheep industry, the pronghorn population is now about one million.

controls on the free grazing of livestock did the rest. The pronghorn population is now considered stable at about one million.[12]

The white-tailed deer actually benefited from the cutting down of forests. The second growth that appeared made excellent food for them. They flourished along highways and at the edges of large land developments. Strict hunting regulations in all states and the decline in predators such as wolves have also helped them.

Deer have invaded many suburbs and are considered a nuisance by many homeowners, whose expensive shrubs they eat almost as soon as they are planted. Hunting regulations have been eased in some states to keep the population down. The return of predators like the wolf and the mountain lion may also keep their numbers under control.

The white-tailed deer's cousin, the Florida Key deer, has not been as lucky. These small deer are protected in a refuge in south Florida and have not been hunted since 1939. Their habitat, however, is crisscrossed with roads and highways. Florida Key deer are often accidentally hit by motorists. As many Key deer are killed every year as new ones are born.[13]

*T*he white-tailed deer is one of the few animals that actually benefited from the cutting down of forests. Because of the decline in their natural predators, they now face the problem of overpopulation.

Chapter 6

What Needs to Be Done

Wildlife protection and conservation have improved greatly since the beginning of the wildlife conservation movement in the 1920s. Many of the successful methods for preserving animals and their habitats have become standard practices. A system of protected areas such as national parks, wilderness areas, and wildlife refuges stretches from coast to coast.

National parks are well known for their conservation of wildlife and natural environments. They are, however, intended mainly to provide the public with a natural setting for recreation, education, or relaxation. Wilderness areas and wildlife preserves are devoted to preserving, protecting, and maintaining animal and plant species. Members of the public are welcome to visit them but are not encouraged to use these areas as they would a national park. The government has made animal and habitat preservation a national policy through the Endangered Species Act. The general public has indicated its support. Animals are no longer widely thought of as creatures in the service of humankind, to be used as needed and then destroyed when they become inconvenient or get in the way.

Despite all of the improvements, there are still about five hundred endangered or threatened animal species on the government's list. There are hundreds more waiting to be added. The rapid growth in human population and human needs seems to have doomed a good portion of the nation's living creatures.

One of the simplest and most obvious things we can do to preserve and protect some animals is just leave them alone. The gray whale off the coast of Southern California, for example, has survived and even prospered all on its own. The only thing humans had to do was stop killing them. In 1994, the gray whale became the first and only endangered marine animal to be taken off the endangered list.[1]

"Hands On" Management

Another thing that we can do is take part in active, "hands on" management of animals' habitats. Hands-on management means protecting or improving the habitat. This can be done, for example, by destroying weeds that may have been introduced from outside the habitat and that threaten its native plants and animals.[2]

With modern means of transportation, it is easy for the seeds of a plant from another continent to find their way to this country. Sometimes these alien plants can take over a habitat.[3] An example is the kudzu vine, an Asian plant that is rapidly taking over whole areas of the South. This vine has deprived wildlife of necessary vegetation.[4]

A popular form of hands-on management is the cleanup campaign. Many communities make Earth Day an occasion for cleaning up places such as vacant lots and parking areas. The "Adopt a

▶What You Can Do

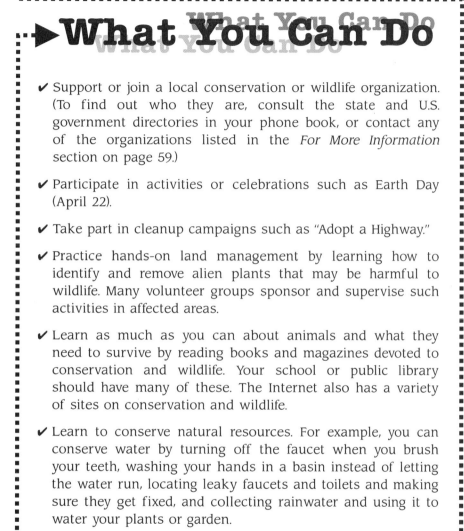

✔ Support or join a local conservation or wildlife organization. (To find out who they are, consult the state and U.S. government directories in your phone book, or contact any of the organizations listed in the *For More Information* section on page 59.)

✔ Participate in activities or celebrations such as Earth Day (April 22).

✔ Take part in cleanup campaigns such as "Adopt a Highway."

✔ Practice hands-on land management by learning how to identify and remove alien plants that may be harmful to wildlife. Many volunteer groups sponsor and supervise such activities in affected areas.

✔ Learn as much as you can about animals and what they need to survive by reading books and magazines devoted to conservation and wildlife. Your school or public library should have many of these. The Internet also has a variety of sites on conservation and wildlife.

✔ Learn to conserve natural resources. For example, you can conserve water by turning off the faucet when you brush your teeth, washing your hands in a basin instead of letting the water run, locating leaky faucets and toilets and making sure they get fixed, and collecting rainwater and using it to water your plants or garden.

Highway" programs that have started in almost every state are useful, easy, and even fun ways to improve human as well as animal habitats. They also make good school or club projects for teenagers. Of course, be sure to take any appropriate safety precautions while working on such a project.

Fire

In the past, state governments did everything they could to prevent or control forest fires. Biologists now believe that this kind of control may be harmful to certain habitats. Forest fires caused by lightning storms and dry spells are natural events. The burning off of undergrowth and old or dead wood helps to keep forest habitats healthy. So another example of hands-on management would be controlled burning within certain areas, which would then be allowed to rebuild themselves.

There is nothing in the Endangered Species Act that requires landowners to take such action.

*F*orest fires that are caused by natural events can be dangerous, but they also help keep forest habitats healthy by burning off undergrowth and dead wood.

Indeed, some landowners find they can remove an endangered species from their property by simply letting the habitat become unsuitable for the animals that live there. Once the endangered animal is gone, the landowners are free to do with the land what they wish. Conservationists would prefer instead to see large-scale landowners rewarded for proper management of their land.[5]

Antipollution Laws

Pollution has always been a threat to animals. All state governments have active antipollution laws. Much of the pollution that threatens animals, however, comes from agricultural runoff. These are materials that sink into the earth or into rivers and streams, such as silt, chemicals, and extra nutrients. The pollutants cannot be pinpointed and therefore are difficult to control.[6] No single farm in Kansas, for example, could be held responsible for the pollution of all the state's lakes and rivers. Science, technology, and industry must find some way to solve this problem. If they do not, the future effects on both animals and people could be disastrous.

Education

Many efforts have been made to increase public education and awareness of conservation issues. Our educational system has devoted special programs to conservation, particularly in connection with Earth Day. Teaching others about the need to respect and protect wildlife and the environment may be the greatest hope for wildlife, now and in the future.

Organizations

National Audubon Society
1901 Pennsylvania Avenue NW
Washington, DC 20006
(202) 861-2242

National Wildlife Federation
1400 16th Street NW
Washington, DC 20036
(202) 797-6800

The Nature Conservancy
4245 N. Fairfax Drive, Suite 100
Arlington, VA 22203
(703) 641-5300

Wilderness Society
1615 M Street NW
Washington, DC 20036
(202) 833-2300

World Wildlife Fund
1250 24th Street
Washington, DC 20037
(202) 293-4800

Web Sites

The United States Fish & Wildlife Service
<http://www.fws.gov>

The United States Fish & Wildlife Service provides a full range of sites on the Internet for anyone interested in conservation and endangered animals.

**The National Endangered Species
Act Reform Coalition**
<http://www.nesarc.org>

The National Endangered Species Act Reform Coalition provides information and news on the Internet for farmers, ranchers, developers, and others who are most affected by the Endangered Species Act.

Chapter 1. The Problem

1. Douglas H. Chadwick and Joel Sartore, *The Company We Keep: America's Endangered Species* (Washington, D.C.: National Geographic Society, 1996), p. 26.

2. Roger L. DiSilvestro, *The Endangered Kingdom: The Struggle to Save America's Wildlife* (New York: John Wiley & Sons, 1989), p. 198.

3. Jane E. Brody, "Once Near Death, a Comeback Bird Thrives in Cities," *The New York Times*, February 15, 2000, pp. F1, F4.

4. "After 30 Years, the Nation's Living Symbol Is Deemed Safe," *The New York Times*, July 3, 1999, p. A8.

5. Chadwick and Sartore, p. 119.

6. Ibid., p. 38.

7. DiSilvestro, p. 14.

8. Chadwick and Sartore, p. 38.

9. DiSilvestro, p. 8.

10. Mary Shurstack, "Hall of Biodiversity," *Weekend*, May 28, 1998, p. F3.

11. "Unendangered List," *Time*, May 18, 1998, p. 34.

Chapter 2. From Destruction to Conservation

1. Roger L. DiSilvestro, *The Endangered Kingdom: The Struggle to Save America's Wildlife* (New York: John Wiley & Sons, 1989), pp. 22–23.

2. Ibid., p. 23.

3. Ibid., p. 64.

4. Douglas H. Chadwick and Joel Sartore, *The Company We Keep: America's Endangered Species* (Washington, D.C.: National Geographic Society, 1996). p. 94.

Chapter 3. The Greatest Threats

1. Robert M. McClung, *Lost Wild America: The Story of Our Extinct and Vanishing Wildlife* (Hamden, Conn.: Linnet Books, 1993), p. 77.

2. Aldo Leopold, *Game Management* (New York: Charles Scribner's Sons, 1933), p. 8.

3. Ibid.

4. David S. Wilcove, et al., "Quantifying Threats to Imperiled Species in the United States," *BioScience*, August 1998, p. 616.

5. Ibid., pp. 607–616.

6. Edward O. Wilson, *The Diversity of Life* (Cambridge, Mass.: Harvard University Press, 1992), p. 280.

Chapter 4. The Politics of Endangerment

1. "Migratory Bird Treaty Act," *Federal Wildlife Laws Handbook*, July 3, 1918, <http://www.fws.gov./laws/federal/summaries/mbta.html> (March 16, 2000).

2. "Bear River National Wildlife Refuge," U.S. Fish and Wildlife Service, n.d., <http://www.r6.fws.gov/REFUGES/BEAR/BEAR.HTM> (March 16, 2000).

3. Roger L. DiSilvestro, *The Endangered Kingdom: The Struggle to Save America's Wildlife* (New York: John Wiley & Sons, 1989), pp. 198–199.

4. Douglas H. Chadwick and Joel Sartore, *The Company We Keep: America's Endangered Species* (Washington, D.C.: National Geographic Society, 1996), p. 21.

5. Stewart L. Udall, *The Quiet Crisis* (New York: Holt, Rinehart and Winston, 1963), pp. 185–186.

6. Endangered Species Act (Washington, D.C.: Government Printing Office, 1973), p. 1.

7. Ibid.

8. Chadwick and Sartore, p. 24.

9. Susan Zakin, "Terms of Endangerment," *Sports Afield*, June–July 1998, p. 41.

Chapter 5. Some Successes

1. "Unendangered List," *Time*, May 18, 1998, p. 34.

2. Ted Williams, "Back from the Brink," *Audubon*, November–December 1998, p. 73.

3. Patrick O'Driscoll, "Another Gray Wolf Discovered Dead," *USA Today*, November 25, 1998, p. 20.

4. Williams, p. 74.

5. Ibid., p. 76.

6. Ibid., pp. 72–73.

7. Rick Lyman, "Government Weighs Protection for Prairie Dogs," *The New York Times*, January 12, 1999, p. A10.

8. Williams, p. 74.

9. Douglas H. Chadwick and Joel Sartore, *The Company We Keep: America's Endangered Species* (Washington, D.C.: National Geographic Society, 1996), p. 108.

10. Roger L. DiSilvestro, *The Endangered Kingdom: The Struggle to Save America's Wildlife* (New York: John Wiley & Sons, 1989), p. 125.

11. Jane E. Brody, "Once Near Death, a Comeback Bird Thrives in Cities," *The New York Times*, February 15, 2000, pp. F1, F4.

12. DiSilvestro, p. 58.

13. Chadwick and Sartore, p. 102.

Chapter 6. What Needs to Be Done

1. Ted Williams, "Back from the Brink," *Audubon*, November–December 1998, p. 70.

2. David S. Wilcove, et al., "Quantifying Threats to Imperiled Species in the United States," *BioScience*, August 1998, p. 615.

3. Ibid., p. 613.

4. "What Is Kudzu," n.d., <http://www.mindspring.com/wxrnot/kudzu.html> (January 25, 2000).

5. Wilcove, et al., p. 615.

6. Ibid.

Further Reading

Blashfield, Jean F., and Wallace B. Black. *Endangered Species*. Chicago: Children's Press, 1992.

Carson, Rachel. *Silent Spring*. Boston: Houghton Mifflin, 1962.

DeKoster, Katie. *Endangered Species*. San Diego: Greenhaven Press, Inc., 1998.

Gore, Al. *Earth in the Balance: Ecology and the Human Spirit*. Boston: Houghton Mifflin, 1992.

Halpern, Robert R. *Green Planet Rescue: Saving the Earth's Endangered Plants*. New York: Franklin Watts, Inc., 1993.

McClung, Robert M. *Lost Wild America: The Story of Our Extinct and Vanishing Wildlife*. Hamden, Conn.: Shoe String Press, 1993.

Roberts, Russell. *Endangered Species*. San Diego: Lucent Books, 1998.

Udall, Stewart L. *The Quiet Crisis*. New York: Holt, Rinehart and Winston, 1963.

Vergoth, Karin. *Endangered Species*. New York: Franklin Watts, Inc., 2000.

Index